The
FOUNTAIN *of*
FORGETFULNESS

The
FOUNTAIN *of*
FORGETFULNESS

SHEILA THOMAS

WestBow
PRESS
A DIVISION OF THOMAS NELSON

Copyright © 2013 Sheila Thomas.

All rights reserved. No part of this book may be used or reproduced by any means, graphic, electronic, or mechanical, including photocopying, recording, taping or by any information storage retrieval system without the written permission of the publisher except in the case of brief quotations embodied in critical articles and reviews.

WestBow Press books may be ordered through booksellers or by contacting:

WestBow Press
A Division of Thomas Nelson
1663 Liberty Drive
Bloomington, IN 47403
www.westbowpress.com
1 (866) 928-1240

Because of the dynamic nature of the Internet, any web addresses or links contained in this book may have changed since publication and may no longer be valid. The views expressed in this work are solely those of the author and do not necessarily reflect the views of the publisher, and the publisher hereby disclaims any responsibility for them.

Cover illustration by Lucy Holtsnider.

ISBN: 978-1-4908-1348-6 (e)
ISBN: 978-1-4908-1349-3 (sc)

Library of Congress Control Number: 2013918671

Printed in the United States of America.

WestBow Press rev. date: 10/31/2013

Dedication

This story is dedicated to
Katarina Dovžan Lazar,
Julia Lazar Denike,
and Jeff Heim.
You have inspired me.

Acknowledgments

Thank you, Jim Feely, for helping me get past my 'stuckness.' I also want to thank Gen Quinette and Lynda Seiler Denny for helping me move forward.

Preface

The souls who are speaking cannot be considered male or female. They are souls of the heavenly realm. They encompass all aspects of good, though on earth some are considered as female traits, others as male. Without bodies, there are no physical differences to characterize them as men or women. It seems unkind to refer to a soul as 'it,' thus another pronoun would be needed as a reference. Je, in the Slovene language, refers to all: he/she/it. To conform to English, the possessive would be jes (pronounced 'yes').

Contents

1

The Heavenly

"Ah, I see you are getting restless. You have been speaking of the condition of life that is happening on earth right now. Though you have not been there before, it makes me think you would like to go there now."

"Yes," the soul said softly. "There is trouble there. I may, though perhaps in some small way, ease this trouble."

The souls who were speaking were Esse and Eimi. Esse had been pondering the souls on earth and had begun to feel many of the souls there were troubled.

They appeared to be in a white room. Its whiteness was so brilliant that it was difficult to see where the floor met the wall or the wall met the ceiling. Being souls that had not yet acquired a body, there was no need to place their feet on solid ground. There were, as yet, no feet.

In heaven, the souls are neither male nor female. Each soul is referred to as je rather than he or she, with no regard for the earth-bound distinctions describing male or female characteristics.

There is no will, free or otherwise. Within the Pure Spirit, all are one, and the One is pure goodness. It never occurs to the One to act contrary to this goodness.

There is no time in eternity. On earth, people are born, have lives, and die. In eternity, the being born, the living, and the dying are happening at once.

2

Love

"Why did the Spirit create earth?" asked Esse.

Eimi responded, "The earth is a beautiful place. Mountains, plains, oceans, meadows with streams flowing through them. The earth is another aspect of heaven, a place meant to nourish souls with its glory. It was also desired that it would be a place where the souls would be stretched, grow, and become even greater in the love they could offer. To do this, one must have free will to make choices in which a soul may become greater in love. So there must be choices to be made and a will to make these choices. Lately, I am feeling that many of the choices being made by the souls on earth are moving them away from love, not toward it."

"Can you describe love?"

"In its basic form, love means that one wishes well for another. One accepts the other for who that person is. It is not jealous or unkind. A person sincerely hopes the other will have sufficient resources: food, clothing, shelter, personal love, friendships, spirituality, the good things in life. It is not necessary to like the other person, just simply that one wishes what is best for the other. This is the love one can feel for anyone.

"The most complete form of love is unconditional love. This is the love of the Spirit. It is affection without limitation, a love based simply on the existence of the other. It is nonjudgmental, even when the other makes mistakes or chooses a path different from the one wished for that person. The one who loves continues to give, even when nothing is expected in return. The one being loved does not need to be anything other than who one is at each moment in life. This love is unchanging. It is an egoless love. It is complete acceptance, with no boundaries.

"It is seldom that unconditional love can be found on earth. Boundaries exist there. Requiring freedom from abuse and neglect is an important boundary. The Spirit does not need these boundaries. One can neglect or abuse the Spirit, but the Spirit can take it. One can be angry with the Spirit, but the Spirit still smiles on the person.

"The closest one can come to unconditional love on earth is often seen between a parent and a child.

"There are other forms of love.

"There is self love, which is necessary. One must care for and nurture one's self before one can care for, nurture, honor and love another.

"There is a general love of all of humanity even if one does not know the other. It may take on the task of volunteering for a cause that helps the community or the world. This love is making the world a better place for all.

"There is a love for a specific other. One cares about another without letting the individual's own personal agenda or self-needs get in the way. One appreciates and celebrates the other, caring about, cherishing and taking delight in the person.

"There is intimacy: a trust and loving of another where the people share thoughts, feelings, and experiences jointly. This may grow into a long-term commitment where the people share understanding. They are willing to compromise so that the good of both are met.

"Real love does not turn into hate in the heat of a moment. Or a temporary bump in the relationship. Real love is abiding. While bumps on the road occur, love remembers there is something more, something deeper. The bumps seem less significant, less real, than the continuity of continued cherishing.

"There is a shared history in intimate love that sustains people through these bumps. Trust is needed. Trust in the shared history. Trust that the other person is not being deliberately hurtful. Trust that one may not always understand the other person, but accepts the person anyway. Trust that the other will trust one back even if the individual is not at one's best.

"Love shows itself through kindness, generosity, and self-sacrifice. Love is working through difficulties and lifting people up. Love gives and receives.

"Another form of love is devotion to the Spirit. On earth, there are stages when growing love for the Spirit:

> Love self for self's sake.
> Love the Spirit for self's sake.
> Love the Spirit for the Spirit's sake.
> Love self for Spirit's sake.

"The first stage shows it is necessary to love one's self before one can love another. Petition and intersession are loving the Spirit for one's own sake or the sake of others, but it is not a love of the Spirit for the Spirit's sake. Hardship and a feeling of abandonment by the Spirit often mark the journey between the second step and the third. People feel a dry time. They are not feeling connected to the heavenly. They feel they are walking alone. One must keep on praying through the dry times, keep on lifting up the people around one.

This is also a time when one will need to be lifted up by others. This part of the journey requires patience, waiting, acceptance, and faith.

"When a person achieves the third stage, one will love the Spirit completely. One will no longer bargain with nor distrust the Spirit. Praise and thankfulness for the Spirit are untouched by any concern for the self.

"In the last stage, one will love one's self as the person dedicates one's life to the Spirit.

"There is a romantic, passionate feeling called love. This is not real love. This attraction may become love if it transforms itself into a genuine intimacy."

"How does this love grow?"

"Joyfully accept the journey on earth. Appreciate the wonders that are available. Life is not a journey from 'here' to 'there.' It is a twisting and turning set of events with many side trips that add color and depth along the way. It is unpredictable, beautiful, ugly, enhancing. A never-ending set of discoveries. A place where love can grow.

"Seek love from one's own personal relationship with the Spirit. Place that growth within a proper context. Withdraw from the ego and the ego's needs but be vibrantly alive and present. Work at loving the Spirit, the earth, all of its people, all of creation. Live in the Spirit. The Spirit will gently urge one on.

"One can accomplish much by listening to the Inner Voice. Or by a walk in the woods. Or in solitude. Growth in love can also be accomplished as the result of the souls on earth making it happen. A beautiful picture, an inspiring book, a gentle presence for another person. Souls reaching out to one another. Loving one another. Sharing the fruits of other's labor, giving back what one can.

"To move upward in love, one must not be judgmental of others. Hold nothing against anyone. Do not label others. Listen thoughtfully as another shares thoughts, feelings, perceptions.

"Be at peace with relationships, past and present. It takes a lot of energy to continue the path of anger. If one can forgive, this energy can be used elsewhere. Forgiving will move one away from this prison of anger, which prevents a person from loving.

"Remain cheerful and positive, undefeated, still celebrating life even as one is presented with challenges. A challenge is not a cross to bear, but an opportunity to explore. Challenges bring people into new ways, which they would not have done without the challenge. They had been complacent with the old ways. A known challenge is easier to bear because one is familiar with it and has learned to cope with it. The new challenge breaks one away from this complacency and may cause a person to grow."

Esse asked, "Can you explain a bit more?"

Eimi answered, "The human condition tends toward complacency, sometimes laziness. Adversity shakes one out of this. Life's problems seem bigger than life, but they are phantoms of some sort. If a person positions one's self correctly, the problems will sail over the person and disappear. The Spirit will give the individual the grace and strength to carry the person through.

"When a soul has grown as fully as je can in love, je gets subsumed into the Oneness of the Spirit."

Esse said, "So I see there is a chance we can become more loving by our encounter on earth. But why go to earth at all? Isn't the love we currently have in heaven enough?"

Eimi answered, "Like eternity, there is also infinity. Our love is ever-expanding. Time on earth is one way we can expand our love and grow the infinity."

3

The Earthly

"This love is wonderful," said Esse. "Why, then, do the souls on earth turn away from this love, and from the Spirit?"

Eimi began. "In the beginning, souls went to earth to glorify the Spirit in the beauty of the earth. However, they also wanted to be in control of their lives. They started to make choices to satisfy their earthly egos rather than conforming to the Oneness of the Spirit.

"The earthly body needs nourishment. Hunters and gatherers collected food. They need shelter, so they devised ways to house their bodies. After a time, people saw some were more successful than others. This gave way to envy. There were people who wanted what another person had. There were choices to be made. A community could be formed. Sharing could occur. There would be no need to feel guilty by those less fortunate when accepting the offerings of those who were more fortunate. Those receiving would give back what they could, using their own particular gifts. Or pride could take over. The beginning of the haves and the have-nots could begin. Unfortunately, this latter choice became more frequent than the former. This turning of the self to the earthly joys started the path that has made many people isolated from the Spirit, and toward the anguish that is now seen on earth. In doing so, the earthly joys also became less frequent.

"The more the earthly joys diminished, the more people wanted greater control over their lives. They wanted to try to get the earthly joys back. They turned away from the Spirit and relied more on themselves. Their spiritual lives suffered.

"People began to fight in order to get what others had, and which they wanted for themselves. They suppressed others, enslaved others, to get what the ego-self wanted. Along the way, they got into businesses. Some of their workers were oppressed in order to get more earthly joys for the owners.

"Pride in one's possessions became important. People wanted to 'keep up with the Joneses.' They became even more envious of what others had. They became greedy. With all of this, people created suffering for others."

Esse began to think about this suffering. Je wondered how a person could overcome it. As though

Eimi could read Esse's thoughts, Eimi offered, "The suffering can be overcome through forgiveness."

Esse said, "Please describe forgiveness."

Eimi responded, "It is perceived that you or someone has been harmed in some way. Someone else is blamed for the harmful behavior. That person is seen as guilty. If you are angry or frustrated with that person, it damages your lovingness. Forgiveness is the solution. Forgive for yourself. Forgive in your heart. You will become more whole.

"One may hate what another has done, but will not hate the person. While one does not condone the behavior, one must try to understand it. Focus on the offender's humanity, not just the hurtful behavior.

"Forgiveness does not need the involvement of the other party. You do not need to tell the offender. Remorse on the part of others, and an apology, may help, but these are not necessary.

"For people, forgiveness is a process. It does not happen all at once.

"Pray for those for whom you want to forgive. You can begin these prayers in anger, but still wish for them all of the spiritual gifts you would want for yourself. Picture both of you surrounded by the Pure Spirit.

"When you forgive, the anger and pain will be

transformed into compassion for yourself and for the other.

"Although je is always forgiving, it may be helpful for a person to ask the Spirit for this forgiveness. In this case, the person will focus on an action one has performed, and which was unloving. Asking for forgiveness brings to mind the need to change one's ways so this action will not happen again. It may be helpful to ask for the grace and strength to make things as right again as one can."

4

Loss of the Spirit-self

ESSE BECAME THOUGHTFUL, THEN QUESTIONED, "WHY does this get perpetuated? Why don't earthly souls turn back to the Spirit and away from the earthly desires you mentioned earlier?"

Eimi replied, "People are shackled by their culture, by traditions, by the limited truth of their elders. They are born knowing the Spirit, feeling je. But they are usually dissuaded of this way of knowing and feeling je by adults, whose concept of the Spirit has also been damaged by their elders. Many adults conceptualize the Spirit as something other than the caring, loving Presence. Or they deny that there is a Spirit at all.

"Many of these ideas are learned at the hands of the parents. A child may ask about the God of the parents and be told 'You must not question. Just believe as I do.' Or the child may be told 'Do as I say, not as I do.' The parents may punish the child if the child does not conform to the parent's ideas. They may suggest the child will go to an everlasting hell, with no chance of redemption. An eternity of suffering. The child begins to doubt its own spirit. It tries to conform to the dictates of its parents.

"Not that the parents are wrong in disciplining their children when the childish ways are misguided. It is when the child's ways are good, but the parents or guardians disregard the Spirit within the child. They try to conform the child to the will of the caretakers and therefore discipline the child away from the desires of the Spirit. As a way to avoid this, one might ask the child what is meant, and so may learn from the little one.

"People often fail to see the divine revelation that is given to them. There are times when it is appropriate to listen to the wisdom of the elders. There is also a time to listen to the wisdom of the generation to come, who have moved past traditions and on to a greater understanding of the desires of the Spirit."

"There is much to absorb," said Esse. "I need a space in which to ponder all you have told me."

The souls were in silence. Esse considered all that had been told to je. Then je spent a moment praising and glorifying the Spirit in true love. But Esse was still unsure of so many earthly things.

"I am sure many parents mean well. They must want what is best for their children. They would want to bring their children to the God of their religion. Though you say some of it moves the child away from the desires of the Spirit."

"There are many misguided notions of conforming to the Pure Spirit. One may believe a person must give at all costs to others, saying 'yes' to the many demands being made of the individual in family, civic, or community life. People are judgmental of others for not performing to their expectations. The person is filled with the 'shoulds' of other's desires, whether these desires are of the Spirit or not. They try to fulfill this role of 'shoulds.' They become critical of themselves when they cannot meet the demands of this role.

"There was a woman who built a snowman for the delight of her neighbor. The neighbor gave the snowman a name and a personality. She made him judgmental of her smoking and other lifestyle choices. The first woman said she thought the snowman looked pretty accepting. She thought he would not be critical. After all, a fantasy friend should be perfect. However, the neighbor kept slipping into the critical. How easily one gives in to self-criticism that one unnecessarily aims at one's self, learned at the hands of another.

"One is best ignoring the constant chatter of one's mind about all of the personal 'shoulds.' It is a waste of time and energy trying to fulfill these. Instead, try to find that which the Spirit wants of one in the next step of life. Sense the Spirit from one's individual potential. Develop that potential as fully as one can. Make the most of the gifts, talents, skills, and energy one has. People contribute from where they are. Bloom where you are planted; bloom where you are transplanted."

"Adults also have a way of moving away from the spirit-self in them. How does this happen?"

"It is the egotistic self that gets in the way of many people. They desire to control their lives instead of letting the Spirit be in control. This keeps many people from reaching the spirit-self in them. It also causes them to try to control the people and situations around them.

"Worries may keep one from the Spirit. If one gets so caught up in worrying about the details of daily life, one may stifle the spiritual life.

"Denial is a great way of removing oneself from the divine. Deny the ego-self is imperfect. Deny the promptings of the spirit-self. Deny that earthly truth is incomplete. Deny the opposite, that the other side may have some truth in it. Deny that people can come lovingly together to a greater understanding of a situation. Deny that if each side lets go of its own idea of truth, they will find a new way of seeing Truth.

"Disappointment may move people away from the Spirit. How often I have heard people say 'If I were God, I would…' How egotistical to think the Spirit has less of an understanding of what is right and good than this person has."

5

The Ego-self

"WHAT ARE ASPECTS OF THE EGO-SELF?" ASKED ESSE.

Eimi replied, "There is a desire to be loved. A desire for independence, freedom, health, security. For some, there is a desire for power, wealth, fame, or control. There is a desire for having sexual needs met. For many, there is a desire for perfection, perhaps if only in the sight of others. There is fear, concern, hope, and despair. There is joy, resignation, and a soaring of the spirit.

"Each person is his own universe. He is the 'I' at the center. He can imagine another's thoughts and feelings but it is always filtered through this 'I,' from the lens of his own experience.

"This 'I' is both the soul and the ego. It is formed through both nature and nurture. The soul was there before life began. This is the natural part of the person. The individual is also nurtured by people and events during his earthly life. These external forces are both positive and negative. For example, a father's love will guide the child in a positive way. The mother's alcoholism may have a negative affect on the child. Though in life, if the person comes to terms with it, the individual can become more compassionate because of this experience.

"At the center of one's life, one has thoughts and feelings one does not share with another. A person would be boring if every thought was expressed. If this were so, one would never stop talking because thoughts keep flowing.

"In the inner circle of one's friends, one shares interests, thoughts, and feelings. Then there are acquaintances. Perhaps these are the people with whom one works. Pleasantries are shared but not deep personal information. Beyond this are people who are known, perhaps a store clerk or someone who is only known through media exposure. At the outer circle of one's life, there are people that one knows are there though they are unknown to that specific individual.

"In his universe, he must recognize that these other people are his suns, moons, and stars that make his universe better. And he is in their universes. It is helpful to be a good sun, moon, or star in the lives of others.

"There is no altruism. If one performs a good action for another, it is because one wants a better world. This is seen as a better place for the individual who is doing good. This is not a bad thing. It is simply a part of earthly life.

"The ego-self can get in the way of the spirit-self."

"People can become wounded by their experiences on earth. How does one embrace the wounds and offer them to the Spirit for healing?"

"People may be emotionally or mentally wounded. These wounds come from the abuse, neglect, or violence they have experienced. Sometimes it is obvious, as when a person repeatedly tells another that they are unworthy of love. There are also subtle ways in which people violate the beingness of another.

"People often try to hide or bury their wounds. If they do, these wounds will fester within them, causing suffering for themselves and others. Or one can share these wounds with others. The love of another earthly soul, the spirit-self of this person, can become a source of healing.

"One may examine the wound. One may face it straight on without blaming the one who caused the suffering. In doing so, the person opens up a space within oneself where the heavenly Spirit can enter and begin the healing. It requires forgiveness in order to transform the wounds into strengths, from pain to compassion."

6

Returning to the Spirit

"THERE ARE TIMES WHEN PEOPLE WANT TO REACH OUT to the Spirit," commented Esse. "They are trying, but they do not seem to find je. Why do they fail to return to the Spirit?"

"They may be trying for the wrong reasons. If one feels the Spirit is to be used to enhance the ego-self, one will be looking for the wrong thing. The Spirit is not what this person will find.

"Sometimes a person tries to find the Spirit by going to various churches. But she brings her willfulness with her, wanting others to think of her as being more important than she thinks of herself. She may lie to get attention, or show off her physical loveliness. This keeps her from finding the Spirit, even in a church, because her ego-self is more important to her than her spirit-self.

"At other times, some may become too fearful of what they may find that they abandon the quest."

"If I go to earth, and people, events, or my own thoughts and actions move me away from the Spirit, how can I get my spirit-self back?"

"When you find yourself moving away from the Spirit, it is helpful to slow down.

"Realign yourself with the Spirit. Explore your inward self. Explore your outward self.

"Ask yourself:

Who am I?
Why am I?
Where have I come from?
Where am I going?

"Seek to understand your higher purpose rather than your immediate comfort or security. Understand that you are on earth for a reason. There is always enough time to accomplish the purpose for which you have gone to earth. The Spirit will move with you. Je will intercede for you if it is necessary. This will often look like a coincidence.

"On earth, your physical, emotional, and mental images affect your ability to move with your spirit-self. The physical state affects emotions, thoughts, and the ability to center. Do not become so tired that you abandon the quest for the Spirit.

"If you recognize your spirit-self, you can attend to

it. Take time for the Spirit. Prepare yourself daily for meeting je. Attend to prayer. One cannot will oneself to a relationship with the Spirit. A person can only open oneself up to this.

"Be able to doubt and question what you have been told. It is necessary for spiritual growth. Search for answers, guidance, direction, a clear Light. Know the Spirit better through others who have touched you. Sometimes the most important people in your life may be ones you have never met, yet what they did in their lives has a profound effect on yours. By the same token, what you do in your life may profoundly affect people you will never know. All of life is connected.

"Praying to the heavenly Spirit will encourage your soul, your spirit, to be more available to you. Acts of loving yourself and others will also help your spirit-self grow.

"You may need to reevaluate your priorities to keep them in line with your spiritual and loving growth. Do not become too strongly attached to your own wants and desires.

"Many difficulties seem to come from expectations. Let go of your expectations.

"The continuing challenge is to live in the moment. The more continuing challenge is to live in the Spirit's moment, not your own. You will discover much that is precious at every moment.

"A soul chose to become this particular human being. But this person must cooperate with the Spirit to have a fullness on earth. Without this fullness, the person may become depressed, a hypochondriac or an alcoholic, perhaps commit suicide. They are anxious. They lack trust in the Spirit. There are endless tortures people place on themselves that are not the desires of the Spirit. It is only by turning back to the Spirit that one can overcome the agonies one has placed on one's self. Give each day and the events within it to the Spirit.

"Sometimes the only way to let go of the ego-self is to be immersed in the chaos and pain of life. When in chaos and confusion, one is more open to change and growth. If one is fired in a crucible, it can temper and make one stronger, expanding one's capacity to know joy and love. For many, that which one knows best has been dearly won.

"One may find one's spirit-self in this crucible. Then one will turn to the Spirit within, and the Spirit in heaven, and allow the Spirit back into one's life. The person will then let the Spirit take charge, moving with the Spirit instead of the ego-self of control, pride, judgment. The person may rise out of this chaos and move in whatever new direction one is meant to go. It is best not to scramble to put one's life back the way it was.

"When a person gets stuck, it is best to turn it over to the Spirit."

"What should my own actions be?"

"Engage in right action. The end never justifies the means. For example, a person works for a company and discovers that they are unethical in their dealings with suppliers and customers. The person must decide to engage in this unethical behavior or leave the company. There are practical ramifications if the person looses a job. But if the individual follows the course of right action, moral action, then the practical details will take care of themselves.

"Sometimes when one is faced with a choice, the person feels that the right choice makes one feel like the individual is stepping off of a figurative cliff and into the unknown. It requires a leap of faith. But the Spirit will keep one from falling so far that the person cannot get back up again.

"Daily life can be tenuous and unpredictable. One cannot guarantee the outcome of the day or of the moments within it. One can only work on one's self to do what is right."

"How should choices be made?"

"To transcend self-will in order to conform to the Spirit, one needs discernment. In making these choices, one must understand the difference between the desires of the Spirit and earthly desires. For what may seem best for the individual at the time may not be best in the long run. If one discerns what the Spirit is desirous of and acts on this, one will move the world closer to an ideal place.

"Do not will yourself to a decision. Let go of your agenda. Listen to the perceptions of others. Find the truth in their words. Be attentive to the Spirit. You will be led.

"There is never only one choice. Though you may not always be aware of the alternatives, if you let go of your will and let the Spirit guide you, you will find alternative options available to you.

"If more than one person is involved in the decision, the final choice will bring unity for all of the people involved in the process.

"Not every choice needs discernment. Deciding what to have for breakfast does not need such a heavy undertaking. Choosing a style of clothing is often a matter of personal preference. Discernment matters in areas concerning the growth of love on earth."

7

Concerns About Earthly Life

Esse was quiet for a time. Je needed to digest much of what Eimi had offered. Then Esse observed, "People on earth want to feel secure. They want assurance they will eat. They want to know where they will rest their heads at night. And that the resting place will be safe."

"Yes, it is hard not to give in to the temptations to try to secure one's place in earthly life. People are often fearful and concerned for their earthly, not heavenly, future.

"People cannot buy security. Love is the only true security. It is in relationships, with each other and with the Spirit.

"Give to the pool of humanity, one person at a time. When this person's time of need comes, someone will step out of the pool of humanity. What this person needs will be there.

"Health, wealth, jobs, etc., can pass away, but loving relationships endure.

"One cannot cling to these individual relationships. If one does, it would only drive the other away. The loving relationship would no longer exist. People must give their loved ones space, allowing them to be who they are. One has to let go, and be the best one can be. It is in this letting go of another person that love can flourish, and therefore security is assured.

"Choose experience over financial security, and from the illusion of this false security.

"In earthly life, you may not have what you want, though you will always have what you need. One may need to lose one's material things in order to be free, although that is not what a person would normally want. Separate want from need.

"Do not borrow trouble. Trust that the Spirit will understand. Je will give you the answer, direction, or resources you need at any given moment. It is up to you to recognize and accept it.

"Instead of trying to live securely, try instead to live faithfully. Moving faithfully with the Pure Spirit will keep a person secure."

"There are precious moments on earth. How can one enjoy them without trying to recreate them? They make one feel good. One may try to make these moments happen again."

"The ultimate experience. The once-in-a-lifetime trip. The completely perfect celebration. A family reunion, which will never be the same because someone has passed on. These will never happen again. Be content that they happened once. That you knew the joy of it. That you celebrated it. That it was a gift in your life. A precious gift of love and fulfillment that was graced to you. When something is perfect there, is no need to repeat it and impossible to transcend it. Once is truly enough. If you accept this, you will cherish the moment, knowing it cannot be recreated."

8

Returning to Earth

Esse wondered, "If I go to earth, how will I know I will come back to heaven? What if I fail, if I become so self-centered that I end up in hell?"

"Heaven is not a 'place,'" Eimi said. "There are no places in eternity. Therefore, there is no such place as hell. There is joy in eternity. There is also a space within eternity where suffering exists.

"Souls who have not fully returned to the Spirit suffer when they realize that what they have done on earth has caused suffering. Through the action or inaction of these souls, others began to doubt the Spirit and move away from je. Or they may have oppressed another. They may have brought disaster or other suffering to others.

"They may have engaged in envy or pride. They may have lusted after money, power, or another person. They may have consumed more than their fair share of earth's resources. They may have been greedy. They may have been too lazy to help another. They may have been so angered that they harmed another.

"Although the Spirit is all forgiving, these souls have not yet forgiven themselves. They judge themselves, believing their earthly lives were unworthy of the Spirit who sent them.

"Those who have died and gone to heaven see their selfishness revealed to them. They see the damage it has done. They may want to return to earth to try to make up for the selfishness of their former earthly ways. They return to try to undo the damage that is left behind. In doing so, they may return to heaven and come to the joyful space."

"Is this the only reason a soul returns to earth?"

"There are some souls who have not fully lost their need to will for themselves, to control their lives. They have not yet learned to conform to the desires of the Spirit nor to let the Spirit take control of their individual selves. They return because they want their ego-selves to be in control.

"Others return because they are concerned, as you are, with the condition of life on earth, even though it is not of their own doing.

"Some return because their love for a specific other is so enduring that they want to continue in this intimate love again. This loving also helps to grow the infinity of love.

"Still others return so they may glorify the Spirit in the beautiful place called earth."

9

The Good, the Bad, and the Evil

"YOU SPOKE ABOUT FREE WILL AND CHOICES ON EARTH," said Esse. "Some choices are more loving than others. Some choices cause suffering. There seems to be evil on earth, choices that cause the greatest suffering. Can you explain evil?"

Eimi offered, "People are challenged by many things. Some will be at the will of others, not of heaven. There are all manner of unpleasant happenings on earth that are not the according to the Spirit. War, rape, pillage, the list goes on. These are considered evil.

"Even as people choose to perform destructive acts, and the Spirit is saddened, je will not abandon them. Je will always offer grace, the right course of action, and inner human spirit. Perhaps the person will be willing to answer that and to discover the deeper soul within. If not, the person being acted upon will suffer."

"What about natural disasters? Floods, drought, unbidden fires, hurricanes, tornadoes, tsunamis, avalanches…. There are many things that disrupt the lives of people, but are not caused by the free will of the children of earth."

"Sometimes an individual needs to hit rock bottom before the person can become whole.

"A young child's death creates suffering among those who cherished the child. Accidents or diseases are then seen as evil. But the child itself knew this would happen when it decided to return to earth. The child has inspired others by its existence. It has fulfilled what was meant to be. If the parents and others turn their grief over to the Spirit, they will know the child has gone back to heaven. It is in a better place. The world is a better place because of the existence of the child. People grieve for their own loss. They do not grieve for the loss of the loved one, who has lost nothing.

"In some cases what looks like an 'act of God' is really the result of the free will of the person. Some people may choose to live in an area that has natural physical phenomena that disrupts their lives. This may have been an earthly choice. Or they may have decided on this way of death or disruption before they went to earth. They may have wanted these physical phenomena to turn them away from their desires for earthly joys, to turn them back to the Spirit.

"Perhaps a family wants to live by the water. They purposely choose to build a home near the lake, even though they know the lake sometimes rises. When the lake has risen, and their home is flooded, they curse the Spirit for allowing these natural phenomena to occur. Had they not built their home in this location, this natural disaster would not have happened. The lake would simply rise, as it was meant to do. It would be natural, but no disaster would have occurred. The home of the family would be safe because they had chosen to build it in a more suitable place."

"How do people know if something is good or bad?"

"In the given world, things just are. It is a person's judgment, choices, and actions that help or hinder one's self or others.

"The good and bad are also a cultural concept. People are taught that things are good or bad. Drugs, for instance. The concept of drugs has been taught to be a bad thing. It became associated with substances that altered a person's perception of reality, but which had not been prescribed by a trained physician.

"There are drugs that can heal diseases. They can offer hope to the mentally ill. Doctors trained in understanding and treating bodies can determine appropriate drugs, now assigned the term medication, for healing the body or mind. In this case, drugs are seen as good. Doctors can prescribe medications that actually harm the body as well. In this case, medications are deemed as bad.

"Drugs, as with many other things that are assigned the terms good or bad, are neither. They just are. It all comes down to choices made by free will."

"What is sin?"

"Having the knowledge of good and evil, and knowing they are capable of committing evil actions, people assign sins to that which they think is evil. Some of these are truly evil, such as murder. Other sins are merely the result of a specific culture, not of the Spirit's desire.

"Sin is committed when one believes something is morally wrong, and then consciously chooses to do it anyway. It does not matter if it is actually immoral, only that the person believes it is immoral.

"One will justify the sin, convincing oneself it is okay this time because of some external factor. This makes it easier to justify it the next time. After a while, it may become normal for this person to do it. If it is not a desire of the Spirit, if it harms the lovingness of this person, it will cause suffering. If their actions do not cause suffering, trust the Spirit is with them even though you may not agree with them.

"Sometimes one must become immersed in sin in order to overcome it. This is true when a person is taught that an action is immoral and it is really an earth-bound judgment or custom, not a Spirit-bound desire. In this way, a person may come to understand this action is not immoral. One will be released from an unneeded strain. The person may be released from passing judgment on others for engaging in the activity.

"Perhaps a person is taught that it is immoral if one does not attend a church every Sunday. She goes to church out of a sense of obligation, though her heart is not in it. She repeats the words of prayers by rote. She may be proud of herself for attending. But she has been told so many things about the God of her church that she cannot feel any connection with Him. She does not feel the Spirit.

"One Sunday, she sinfully refused to go to church. She feels liberated. It sets her on a process wherein she begins to feel there is a true Spirit. She begins to read about the Spirit and to search for her own soul. She is joyful that she is discovering her spirit-self.

"Through a new understanding of this heavenly Spirit, she now sees the value of attending a church. A community shares her joy of the Spirit. It helps move her closer to the Spirit, and she in turn helps them. Now she attends church, though with no obligation to attend every Sunday, because she feels a connection with the Spirit. She knows that those who do not attend every Sunday are not sinful. They are simply finding their own way back to their souls."

They waited in silence as Esse pondered these words.

10

Truth, Faith, and Prayer

Esse began the conversation again. "Can you tell me about truth?"

"It is all true. There are two sides to a coin. There are also two sides to a truth. While there is some black-and-white in life, it is mostly shades of grey.

"There is a story of a man who asked his spiritual guide if it was okay if he ate while he prayed. He was told this was not okay. When praying, one should devote all of one's attention to prayer. Another man asked if it was okay to pray while he ate. He was told this was okay, because one should pray without ceasing in all that one does. Some people need to steer to the left of the path; others need to find out what is on the right before they can come to a center of truth.

"Speak truth. Do this lovingly. First, it is your truth, not the Ultimate Truth. It may be divine revelation, but it is not the full Truth of heaven. Speaking truth without consideration for another may be hurtful. Their truth may not be the same. Listen to their truth as well. You may learn from it."

"What is spiritual faith?"

"People are composed of physical, emotional, mental, and spiritual aspects. When people are fully whole, these aspects are drawn together so that they are one.

"Most people pull from one or the other at the expense of the rest. Physicians seem to mostly see the physical side. Counselors focus on the emotional. Teachers see the mental side as the most significant. This is still the 'I' stuff not the 'Thy' stuff. People confused emotion or mental activity with spirituality. The spirit side, not the mind, emotions, or the physical, make up our faith.

"The Spirit is not logical or theological. These are of the mind. The Spirit is a different aspect of being. Je can be found in experiences and the still, small voice within. The mind may get in the way of experiencing the Spirit.

"Faith is belief in the Spirit and moving with integrity in je. Integrity is not being consistent with one's past actions. It is moving with the integrity of the Spirit in a single moment. As one's understanding of the Spirit grows, one will be moved to a different course of action. The integrity of the individual is enhanced. The person becomes more integrated.

"Faith is a great gift the Spirit has given to earthly beings, but it would not exist without free will."

"What is the role of the Spirit on earth?"

"The Spirit is within people, the internal spirit-self. Je is also outside of people, the external Pure Spirit. Je surrounds the individual, the community, and all of creation. The Spirit can be felt in jes presence. All of creation is loved. It is safe in the Spirit. People will feel this safety if they allow themselves.

"The Spirit is completely understanding and loving. Je never stops caring about people. Nor does je turn away from them, though people may stop caring about the Spirit.

"Disappointment at events in life may cause people to turn away. They may petition their image of a God. They may intercede for another. If they feel the petition or intersession has not been heard or has not been answered in a way they wanted or expected, they doubt that their image of the Spirit is real. Do not intercede for yourself or for others. Do you not trust the Spirit knows better than you what should happen for your sake or for the sake of others?

"At other times, people become so self-centered that they care only for themselves. They stop caring for others or for the Spirit.

"What the Spirit desires is that people will grow in love, nurture each other, and return to the Pure Spirit. Je will do jes best to help this happen on earth."

"What is prayer?"

"Prayer is a connection with the Spirit. The earthly souls open themselves up to this connection. It is a conscious action that keeps a person open to understanding the desires of the Spirit. It is attentiveness to the Pure Spirit. It is an inner listening. It is an outer action of connection with the divine. Enjoying and appreciating life is a significant spiritual connection.

"Stay conscious of this connection, whether openly praying or simply feeling the oneness a person shares with the Spirit. It may take on the form of frequent 'stops' during the day to thank the Spirit for the gifts je has given.

"Give thanks when you feel it. Offer praise when you mean it. Worship.

"The resistance to pray is sometimes real. Question your ideas and seek the guidance of others when you need it. It may be in person or through books, movies, poems, art, community, or history.

"Practicing disciplines are also prayers. One may engage in lectio divina, meditation, fasting, journaling, and in witness to the Spirit in daily life.

"If one prays for help, this help cannot be for material gifts. The material includes the body and its health. It also cannot be for gifts of prestige, wealth, earthly importance. Instead, the help that will be given is of the spiritual kind.

"The Spirit knows what people need. Je helps people through their time on earth, always ready to give guidance, support, and nurture. It is not necessary to pray to the Spirit for earthly gifts.

"Examples of helping prayer may include:

Please help me know that You ARE helping me.

Please help me understand what You want me to do in each moment.

Please help me understand that You ARE in each moment.

Please help me stop thinking I have control over my life.

"One can pray to the spirit in each person because there is that of the Pure Spirit in all. People may pray each person will be open to the desires of the Spirit and to jes leadings. It is attentiveness to the spirit of other souls on earth. It may help them move away from the ever-present ego and move them closer to the Pure Spirit. This is also a helpful way to pray."

11

Inspiring

Esse wondered, "If I go to earth, would it be possible that I could help ease some of these earthly troubles? Will my going there make any difference?"

Eimi answered, "It will depend on the choices you make, the goals that you seek while on earth. If they are of the Spirit, you will make a positive difference in the earthly lives of other souls."

"You are saying that earthly souls are meant to follow the Spirit. What does this entail?"

"Lay the personal will aside. Let go of self-indulgence. Do not determine the conditions of your life as good or evil. Listen to the Spirit so you can understand. Follow jes desires rather than your own will. Place complete trust in the Spirit.

"Try to find the right blend of action and of being led. In this way, you will truly live the life you and the

Spirit meant for you. You may need to let go of what you planned for today. Instead, do what the day has given to you. Try to live without attachment to whatever tomorrow may bring. This requires not only patience, it also requires faith, joyfulness, good works, and a striving to improve your self for the greater glory of the Spirit. If you are not joyful, you are not doing what you were meant to do.

"Seek balance, harmony, compassion, and love. Achieve an innocence that is beyond naiveté. Be aware of the world and life around you but remain innocent of what may trap you from the desires of the Spirit.

"Forgive yourself when you are unable to fulfill these desires of the Spirit. Your life will not end when you discover you have made a mistake or when you know you have sinned. In your finite form, you will make mistakes or perceive things incorrectly at times. At times, you will sin. Pick yourself up, right things as best you can, and go on.

"The Spirit will not judge you. And earthly beings have no right to judge you nor do you have the right to judge anyone else for mistakes that are made. The only sort of being that has the right to judge is someone who has never made a mistake or a poor choice. I have not yet found an earthly soul who has reached this infinite state.

"There was a man in England during the 1600's. He was a son of an English admiral. It was fashionable at that time to wear a sword. This man joined a pacifist church. He questioned the wearing of the sword even though it was a decoration. He asked his spiritual guide if he should remove it in honor of his new convictions or continue to wear it in deference to the courtly customs. His spiritual guide simply told him, 'Wear it as long as you can.'

"This guide was telling him he must come to his own feelings about it. The guide was not judging him. People must follow their own conscience. The man wrestled with it for a while, then decided to remove the sword. It came from his own sense of self, not from a source external to the man and his spirit-self. He followed the Spirit as it was given to him.

"When you follow the Spirit, you will know love, joy, peace, faith, and have self-control. You will offer patience, kindness, gentleness, and generosity."

"How can I inspire others on earth?"

"You cannot control the free will of others. They will be inspired, uninspired, or your actions of inspiration may not be recognized. You must do what the Spirit desires that you do. Use the gifts the Spirit has given you. Believe in your gifts. It is up to others what their reaction will be.

"To begin, you must find your own center. Then find the spirit in others but do not confine it.

"Behave in the manner in which you believe all people should behave if it is to be a better world. Create a listening ear. Listen with your heart and soul without attending to what you will say next. Lift up others as they falter. Allow others to lift you up.

"When others have lifted you up, there may be no way for you to return the favor to them. Instead, perform an action that helps another person. Your action may be helping someone jumpstart a car. Do not ask for payment for the action. If he offers to pay, tell him the next time it is easy for him do something for someone, do it. Then he will have paid you back though you will not know about it. In this way, you will also have paid back the person who originally helped you.

"People are born to minister to others. Sometimes this is an unconscious ministry. One may not know one is doing it. There are times when the simple presence of a person ministers to another without the person being aware of it. This calls a person to be one's highest self at all times.

"You may be a prism. On earth, you are not a transparent entity wherein the Pure Light pours out. Your Light shines after having passed through your center. You may reflect the Light as it glances off you, no longer pure but now in the colors of a rainbow created by your finite state. Still beautiful but no longer pure.

Colored by your perceptions, your imperfections, your humanity, but easier for others to see because of that.

"When a person must hit rock bottom to become whole, you cannot stand in his way. It is hard to watch this happen. It is even harder when you must be a part of this process. You will want to help him, support him. It may seem un-pure to you to turn your back on him but sometimes this is the most loving thing to do. As long as you are there for him, he will not need to face his brokenness. He may project his brokenness on you, believing the problem is yours, not his. When you are there, you are enabling him to continue in his un-wholeness. You must be strong enough at times to simply walk away, though he and others may be shouting at you to return.

"Let go of your ego-self as much as you can so that you can become a true servant of the Spirit.

"As much as possible, walk cheerfully over the earth. Make a joyful noise unto the Spirit. And sometimes, all you need to do is to be delightful."

"How will I know if I have succeeded in my goals?"

"Provide your best effort. Then let go of the effort and whether or not it succeeded or failed. On earth, you may never know.

"Perhaps your goal is to help another person. Perhaps there is a person anguishing over an event in her life. You sit and listen to this person as she expresses her anguish. No words come to you that would comfort her. Perhaps you feel as though you have failed. But as she goes on with her life, she feels she has truly been heard by your gentle listening. This relieves some of her anguish. Your actions have been successful."

12

Choices

Esse was curious. "If I go to earth, what sort of life will I have?"

"You can have any life that you choose," Eimi said. "There are infinite possibilities. Each is challenging. Earthly life has painful moments and periods of uncertainty. Each life can be rewarding in its own way. Each has the possibility for inspiring the lives around you. They may also put you off track if you are not careful in the choices you make when you are faced with decisions.

"I will spread out some choices. In the end, you will discover for yourself the right life for you.

"There are introverts and extroverts. Extroverts regain their energy for meeting the challenges of each day by being with other people. After a stressful event, they will want to be in community with others. Perhaps a party will meet their needs. Or a long conversation with a friend. They find strength in relationships. An introvert needs to be alone for energy to return. A walk in the woods, taking a nap, sitting on a porch swing. Solitude brings a sense of peace.

"There are conservatives and liberals. Conservatives resist change. They want to preserve traditions, keep the status quo. There is often a sense of security with what is familiar. Liberals prefer reform or progress. As people receive greater understanding of a current condition and feel that it can be improved, they will want to move past the status quo. They want what they believe will be a better situation. Sometimes this may be better, though sometimes the current situation is more loving than the proposed change. Both history and the future are important. It is in the present that the two competing forces can find a common ground.

"There are some who choose mental health challenges. They will see things differently from those who do not have these challenges. If they turn themselves over to the Spirit, they will be given insights that are not available to others. Sharing these insights may inspire others who will then see the world, the people, and the Spirit in a new way. New ways of thinking are needed from this group of people, as well as from all of the other personalities.

"Each personality type is necessary. The differing personalities need each other. A free-spirited person may want to sail openly on the oceans. But he also needs an anchor, someone who will hold him steady at the shore when a storm is upon him.

"Some choose a life of Downs syndrome. These people live in the moment. And the Spirit is always of the moment. It is easier for these people to live in the Spirit.

"Each person is given a life line with individual gifts. One life cannot compare to another except that all are all equal before the Spirit.

"None of these life choices is right or wrong. Each is needed so long as it is not abused."

"What gender would suit me best if I go?"

"One must discern between the two when a soul decides to go to earth. The gender the soul chooses this time may not be the gender the soul chose the last time je went to earth. At times, the best way to fulfill one's role is as a female. At others, the best way is as a male. And some return transgender."

"Can you tell me about life circumstances?"

"Those on earth who are of the generationally wealthy class look to the past, preserving it for themselves and future generations. It is good to remember history, even personal history. But in choosing this path one must remember that personal wealth and history may hamper one from reaching out in love to the poor and downtrodden.

"The generationlly middle class look to the future. They work and save for what will come. The future should not be discounted. But they must be aware that they do not become so concerned for the future of their earthly self and family that they forget to love others.

"There are 3 kinds of poverty: generational, situational, and the chosen.

"The generationally poor look to the present. The Spirit is in the present. Focusing on that presence is beneficial in helping oneself and others. They are very concerned about relationships but it can be at the expense of earning a living or other civic duties. In this path, one must be careful to sustain oneself simply so one does not live at the expense of others.

"This is not the same for those who are poor through unwanted loss of a job, being met with a natural disaster, or being met with a human-made disaster such as war. They do not have the cultural background of those who are generationally poor and so do not have the cultural gift of living in the present. This poverty is more difficult to handle. They see themselves as doing without. They may have mortgages they can no longer afford. Buying groceries may become a problem. They often feel extremely stressed as a result of the poverty. It often creates an even greater need to attempt to control their lives. They often live in a world of private desperation. Out of this can be born a personal desire to get it all back, to try to make sure it never happens again. At its worst, one may stoop to forgery, dishonesty, robbery. Or one may turn one's life over to the Spirit, allowing the Spirit to lead one's life, trusting the Spirit will provide what is needed when it is needed.

"The third type of poverty occurs when one intentionally chooses the vow of poverty. Monks and nuns have done this. They turn away from material possessions so they can focus their attention on the Spirit. There is joy in this type of poverty.

"What you do in earthly life to enhance your heart, mind, and soul will help you as you prepare to return to heaven. Much of your earthly self will revolve around your physical self. You must sleep, which will take about thirty percent of your time. You must eat. This involves growing food, gathering it, preparing it, cooking it, eating it, and cleaning up when you are finished. Most people need clothing. This involves creating material, sewing, laundry, mending, perhaps ironing. You must find, maintain, and clean your shelter.

"Many have jobs so they can afford these things. They do not need to do each step of the process. They shop for groceries so they do not need to farm to gain food. A job takes up a good percentage of time. One would not need a job if one did not have a body.

"In all of this, you must carve out a niche to attend to your heart, mind, and soul. When you work at loving someone, you are enhancing your heart. You may take a portion of you life for education. You may want to tithe your time, reserving a portion of each day engaging in activities to nurture your soul. The dreams in your sleep can also be a source of inspiration for you."

"Is one lifestyle better than others?"

"The best lifestyle is the one that is right for a person at a particular point in time. It is wrong for a person to evangelize about a lifestyle. Statistics and information are important, but they do not apply to all individuals because each body is different. Individual emotional selves are different. Individual minds are different. Each stage of life is different. There is no one-size-fits-all lifestyle that is appropriate."

"You have talked about lifestyles. What about the way of living?"

"There is no one right way of living. However, remember each moment is the Spirit's moment, not that of the ego-self. Do not be lustful of power or money. Any attempt to grab more than you need will push you away from the Spirit. The ego and selfishness will overcome you. Be patient, humble, and obedient to the Spirit.

"When one is in alignment with what one is called to do, a person is joyful. This includes pain along with pleasure. When one is walking the way of the Spirit, the person will be refreshed by jes grace. The individual will be joyful in spite of the difficulty that walking in the Spirit's way may bring.

"You must sing own song, march to the beat of your own drummer, dance your own dance. Accept that others must sing their own song of the Spirit. If you convert them to your song, you will be denying them the ability to sing the song the Spirit meant for them to sing. People can raise their voices to the Spirit together and share the journey. They can blend in harmonies but not distort each other. Rise up singing, and when you do, attend to the songs the Spirit has given each of you uniquely. Let one admire another's song and pray that yours is sung in a worthy manner. You each find your own song. You also need a spiritual community in which you can share it.

"One's concepts of the world, the Spirit, and of one's self may hold a person back. Do not try to adjust the Spirit or heaven according to your expectations. Try not to attach to your concept of what your life should be like. If you get too intent on trying to coerce life to conform to your image of what it ought to be, then you will end up living an imitation of Life.

"It is when one hangs on too tightly – to who one is, to what a person thinks one ought to be - that a person diminishes one's ability to be a vehicle for the creative force of the Spirit in the world."

"How do I live in the world but not of the world?"

"As one seeks to live in the Spirit, one needs to let go of earthly things. It is generally easier if one lives simply. Get rid of the clutter in your life, both material and mental. Do not acquire more material possessions than you need. Handle your to-do list promptly.

"If you have already acquired more than you need because of past actions, get rid of them. You will feel much better when you get rid of the clutter.

"You may need to let go of something you have cherished. You may grieve a bit in letting it go, and the part of your life that it represents. This attachment will no longer exist when you die. You will eventually be glad not to have the attachment any more. One must let go before one can return to the life that is beyond death.

"Remember each moment is a sacrament. Become more attentive of the moments. Stay in the Spirit's moment. Listen for what the Spirit wants from you and for what the Spirit wants for you. Commend your spirit to the Pure Spirit."

"What else can you tell me about earthly life?"

"On earth, you will have some to learn and some to teach. And some to simply experience. It is important to balance the experience of life with the transcendent timelessness.

"Some people desire a crystal ball. If one had this ball, one would see the difficult things coming as well as positive future events. The difficult times would look overwhelming. But as a person works forward through to it, one becomes ready for these things as they happen.

"Life is a process and it is temporary. Do not fight this process. There is the surprise of discovery along life's journey. The delight at coming upon the good things. Anticipation of the unknown rather than the dread of challenges along the way.

"In the world, you will be an imperfect being in an imperfect culture. You will never reach perfection in this earthly form. You may strive for improvement even though it will not be finished during an earthly life. This may keep you humble. It may keep you from being judgmental and self-righteous.

"Accept your self in spite of your earthly imperfections. Only when you accept yourself will you be able to accept others.

"You must choose which form of God will serve you best in meeting your goals. You must decide which religion will best serve you in this matter. Christianity, Judaism, Zen, Islam, the rest. They all ultimately serve the one, true Spirit but the flavors are many. They are suited to different personalities and life circumstances.

"You must choose your death, the shedding of your physical self. Death is only a stage of passing from one form of being to another.

"Each death is different. Most are difficult. Each one gives learning and a greater need for letting go.

"If, in this particular life span, the offering of suffering to meet your goals may be appropriate, you may choose such suffering to meet it. It may be a disease, martyrdom, or suffering the consequences of human action or natural disaster. There are many options. Some are long term, chronic. Some are short term, critical. Within the Christian tradition on earth, examples can be found in their Bible. Chronic suffering was endured by Job. He sets an example of what can be done with long-term suffering. Also in that tradition is a wonderful example of critical suffering as told in the story of Christ.

"If suffering will not help you for yourself or to inspire others in this particular earthly life, you may choose a death that will be easier for you. You may die of old age, perhaps easing out of life while you are sleeping. Or perhaps you may have a heart attack. Or a car accident. This will be easier for you, though it will be more difficult for the people who love you. Because it will be so sudden, your loved ones will not have an opportunity to come to terms with your death prior to its event. But this may also inspire others as they grieve.

"If your goal is accomplished early in this particular life, you may die young. You will return to heaven earlier than many others will. If not, you may stay on earth for a longer time. Also, if you desire extra time on earth in spite of having achieved your goals, it is possible for you to do so.

"It is best to come to terms with your own death while on earth. Your life will be informed by it.

"There are two kinds of experiences in life: the ones that you live through and the one that you do not. The second is the one for which the rest of life is a preparation. The others, whether on the bright side of life or the dark side, will pass away and cycle on to a new set of experiences. You can garner what you can from both the dark and the bright."

13

Spiritual Maturity

"What is spiritual maturity?" asked Esse.

Eimi replied, "It begins with nurturing the space within you, where the spirit is. Open this space so you can experience the Pure Spirit. To know the Spirit, feel jes abiding presence within you and outside of you. Recognize the graces and gifts from the Spirit. Know yourself to be an inseparable part of the timeless and formless.

"Spiritual maturity is being aware at several levels. One pays attention to the task at hand, whether it is driving a car, reading a book, tending a garden. At another level, one is aware that this is the spirit's moment. One offers prayer, thankfulness, and praise to je.

"A spiritually mature person will seek the Light that lives in everyone. The person will feel an inner peace.

"When one is spiritually mature, one will not cling to the past nor be apprehensive of the future. One may dwell in memories and on plans, the past and the future. But the person always stays present in the moment, living one moment at a time.

"In life, one never knows what is just around the next corner. Or whether it will be pleasant or unpleasant. The spiritually mature person will simply be open and ready for anything. The person will patiently move through whatever each day brings, trying to do one's best to meet whatever happens. Do not worry about what the Spirit will want from you. You will know it when you get there. And you will not know it any sooner."

"What do you mean?" asked Esse.

Eimi told a story. "A man and his daughter were talking. The father asked, 'When you are going to get on a train, when do I give you the ticket?' The daughter answered, 'Just when I am about to get on the train. That way, I won't lose the ticket ahead of time.' The father said, 'It is the same way with God. He doesn't give us the ticket for what we are to do next until we need it.'"

Eimi paused as Esse thoughtfully considered what was said. Then Eimi continued.

"Trust that the spirit is leading you to where you need to be next. Know that all is as it should be.

"The Spirit is infinite. On earth, it is difficult to grasp this awesome Being. Many times, the earthly souls feel that are only in the baby steps of finding spiritual maturity."

14

Fountain of Forgetfulness

ESSE PONDERED ALL THAT HAD BEEN TOLD TO JE. Je knew the desire of each soul to help the souls still bound to earth had to be the desire of the individual soul, even as it was gifted to je by the Pure Spirit.

As the soul made the decision to go to earth, a body began to form around je. Ground appeared under the soul because now je had feet, which needed to stand somewhere.

The soul decided to go to earth as a man, one who would grow old while on earth. The body that formed was one of late youth. He had not chosen a handsome body for this particular earthly life, but rather a plain looking one. He did not want to be prideful of his looks. He wondered what he would look like as an infant and how his mother would regard him if he looked less than the ideal child she had imagined.

Gradually a fountain appeared before them.

"Going to earth is a heavy undertaking," said Eimi. "There will be many opportunities to go astray.

"Most people see the world from the perspective of their personal ego. People are bound by this ego on earth, though to what degree is determined by the measure they have drunk from this Fountain of Forgetfulness, of the measure one wants one's free will to conform to the individual rather than to the Spirit.

"To have free will, you must have choices to make. If you take with you all you have come to know in heaven, there will be no choice. You will always know, not discern, what is most loving.

"It is a condition on earth that free will is to be maintained there in order to grow the love.

"There are those on earth who call free will the original sin. It is through the choices one makes that one will live up to the goodness of heaven or conform to selfishness and thus choose to sin. It begins with drinking too deeply from this fountain. But you must drink from it. Without free will, you will not stretch and grow on earth so that you become greater in the love that you have.

"The water is tasty. You are thirsting for it now as you prepare yourself to go to earth. Be cautious, my friend, that you do not drink too deeply. The less you drink, the more you will remember the reason you chose this life and what you are meant to do with it.

"Drink lightly, and you will remember vaguely what you knew before you entered earthly life this time, and what will come to you again as you leave it. This will support you as you move to achieve the goals you are now setting. The lives of humans are endangered because they do not remember what went before they returned to the lovely garden of earth.

"You are thirsty. You must drink from the fountain now."

The man stooped over the fountain. His thirst was great but he remembered all that had been told to him. He took only a short drink. Lifting his face from the fountain, he could feel a desire to control his destiny on earth begin to fill him. He could still vaguely feel the thoughts that had just been given to him, living quietly in the center of his being. If he would only remember to listen to that still, small voice within him, his life on earth will be filled with the Spirit. The earth will then be a better place because he had been there.

15

Moving to Earth

"As you go, I caution you not to forget that the Spirit is always with you and available for you whether you recognize je at the time or not. You must listen carefully for the guiding Spirit. The busyness of earth will try to overtake it. Please do not forget the grace that is in you and around you."

As the man was preparing to go to earth, the Spirit surrounded him. Je lovingly sent him on his way.

In the birthing room at the hospital, the single mother looked down at her newborn son. She had dreaded this moment from the time her boyfriend abandon her, leaving her alone with this new life within her. But as she gazed upon her son, she was amazed. A powerful, wonderful feeling emerged within her. She felt a love she had never known before. Yes, the road ahead looked difficult. But this amazing child she held in her arms, so beautiful in her sight, would make the road ahead a journey worthwhile. Together, they would make the world a better place for having been here.

About the Author

SHEILA THOMAS has been a spiritual seeker all her life. She sought guidance in religious communities, with a spiritual director, on retreats, engaging in spiritual disciplines, and in being inspired by others in her life. This story is a distillation of what she has come to know.